To Martha

Learning to fly is leaping off cliffs
and learning to love is learning to lose
Loved ones we'll miss.

-Hallelujah

To BARBARA

MUCH Love

S Hawk

Original and modified cover art by
Shanden Simmons & Victoria Caldwell

Printed in the United States of America

First Printing, 2018

ISBN 978-0692923849

River City Poetry
Paducah, KY 42001

Ordering Information:
Quantity sales. Special discounts are available on quantity purchases by
corporations, associations, and others.

For details, contact the publisher by email.
Orders by U.S. trade bookstores and wholesalers.
Please contact Big Distribution: via email

www.samuelhawkins.org
samuelhawkins@live.com

the Greatest
stOry
ever solD

the Greatest
stOry
ever solD

HOPE ANCHORED

"Your story is a lightning storm when the lamps go blind."

PART 1 HOPE ANCHORED

Hope—an emotional state which promotes the belief in a positive outcome related to events and circumstances in one's life.

When circumstances are dire life ignites hope's fires. Notice the words positive outcome. What are you reaching for? My father told me that to worry is to pray for undesirable outcomes. By focusing your mind on negative thoughts, you paint the undesired picture of the future you'll catch up to in due time. Hope, on the other hand, paints the masterpiece we can live in tomorrow. Hope is the first step to write the blueprints for a better outcome. Hope is the sum of the mental willpower and way power for your goals. Willpower, that driving force unseen like the wind but it's definitely felt. Pure passion is derived from a divine source. Willpower is much more than blindly going forward. Willpower is doused in wisdom waiting for a creative spark to expel the dark and light the way. Willpower is understanding your goals and how to attain them. Willpower is your parry as well as your punch in the fight for life and what God has to offer.

Way power is using your tools and talents properly to push you forward. If the world builds a wall on the path where success is and you use your ladder as firewood to stay comfortable, you are wasting your resources, time, and talents. Life expires and time is a gift not everyone will receive today or tomorrow. This reminds me of the parable of the talents found in Mathew 25:14-30 of the Holy Bible. The first two servants in the parable doubled what the master gave to them. The last servant dug a hole and casted his talent inside the darkness for no one to see. He did this out of fear. This happens every day. Who do you know that has a talent or two unused because of fear? Fear is the vine that chokes the flower of faith growing from your dreams. Pruning is essential for growth. Negative self-talk and negative people need to be cut out if you wish to rise up. Pursuing your goals is drinking from the cup of life. God is the lighthouse answering your prayers drenched in night thirsty for life. I dare you to ask what's next instead of why. Why would this happen to me? Why can't I give out my trust for free? Why did he molest me? Why did he rape me? Why didn't my mother love me? Why didn't my father come visit me? Why didn't that job call back? Why are the funds low and the bills high? Why is no one listening to me? I dare you to ask God what's next instead of why. I dare you to pick up your cross to crucify your comfortables and fly. Don't ground your faith next to doubtful roots. Ground your faith next to truth. The truth is, you're capable to carry on through this life. Carry on, I believe in you.

Hallelujah

Sunday evening, across the table from my grandmother
This is what she said to me. She said,
"Son, learning to fly is leaping off cliffs
and learning to love is learning to lose
Loved ones we'll miss."

The emptiness will leave the implication
that something was there.
Something is there.

Sometimes, showing strength means
breaking down and kissing the floor
you don't have to hold onto anymore
because God never let go.

I have good news
and I have bad news.
The bad news
God doesn't pick favorites
just obey.

The good news
God doesn't pick favorites
you can just obey
and His love stays.

We all stray, but that was 8,765.81 hours ago.
That's a year by the way, God gave you today.
When you have nothing, you'll find everything.
Heaven bound your eyes to the worries of others.

Don't undercover your mistakes
or they'll echo off your fake
and crumble your faith

like the confidence of cowards
heckling the fears of the courageous.

You can't have courage until you admit you're afraid.
So, be afraid, be very afraid
but eye to eye what you fear most.
Allow the Lord's lips to kiss
the coast of your island of secrets.

Stranded nevermore
leave your comfortables on the shore
take your feet into uncharted waters.
No need to twist the knobs of tomorrow
because God leaves open doors.

If you find yourself on the cliff of regrets
hoping a hang glider will grow from your spine
like your mind, has the power to change reality
it does.

If you're praying
for those winds to never die
like unbroken wedding vows
this poem is for you.

Let's give our faith
to the maestro conducting these winds.
Lift your hands in praise and sing silver hallelujahs.
Your prayers are music to God's ears, Hallelujah!

Have you checked your anatomy lately?
There are bells in that throat.
There's a cathedral in that chest.
Before you start to second guess
No. Uh-uh

The Lord could never learn to love you less.
There was never a need for extravagance or to impress.

There was never a need to coddle comments sent by "cool people"
whose commentary we should actually detest.
You are a living, breathing, walking, rolling,
if need be at times, all of us, crawling miracle.
And you made it this far.

So even when midnight has kidnapped
and convinced your stars to
burn out like faithless candles.
Eternities from now, your daughter's daughter
will witness the glory of your testimony.
So tell the story, of your holy matrimony
to the cross.

I don't write like this because I'm righteous
I write like this because I'm lost.
And I'm hurtin' and I am searching, for hands within the darkness.
I am searching for empathy within the heartless.
I know it exists because, when I gaze deep within the mirror
I see a man, just a broken man not myth or legend so
sing a prayer for me tonight and I'll sing one for you.
And let's give praise like the Heavens are hungry for Hallelujahs
to hang on stars you used to wish on.

Amen.

Cut the Lasso

The rivers of our hearts were not built to hold dams. Holding back is the act of being less than what God intended you to be. It's not as romantic as we'd like it to be. We are mere cogs in a machine. When one refuses to spin in its intended direction, it's hard for all of us to function. Quite simply, we need each other. I need you. Walt Whitman said, "To have great poets you must have great audiences." So this is for every umph, Hallelujah, or finger snap you've given me. You're simply recognizing the greatness you see in yourself and I see it, too. I'm not a poet, I'm a magnifying glass. Let's focus on your past and burn away the ropes holding back your hopes.
This
      Is
            Cutting
                   The
                         Lasso.

Cut the lasso.
Hide your heartbeats in a mason jar.
Tuck them between the sheets of your soul so
before you die, you won't forget that you are
alive. Allow those heartbeats
to bang the bars of sheet music
held together by the trembling treble clef
attached to your last breath.

Lung release those notes.
We all have songs in our chests
and we all have wrongs to confess
and we all long to be the best at something.
You sure are something.

You ain't fooling nobody.
You are much more
yes, much more

than the city skyline
of Texas Hold 'em casino poker chips
pushed all in
on life's poker table.

Don't listen to the broken fables
fed from the mouths of fools
that said your dreams
were better off dead.

They couldn't be more wrong!
C'mon now, cut the lasso!

All of us
are more worthy than we think we are.
All of us
are not as cool as we think we are.

Humble your spirits
to let the light in
and to let the dark out.
Anchor your doubts with the words from my mouth.
You are good enough.
You are good enough.

We all want our lives to mean something.
That's a gift we never had to wait to receive.
All you have to do is unroll that Dragon Scroll
look at your reflection and begin to believe.

So begin to believe and
cut the lasso. Don't hide.
Spotlight your secrets.
Be three again.
And never begin to believe you were never meant to make it.
We all come into this world naked
with only a breath and a heartbeat.
Don't Neosporin the scars on your feet.

They will teach others
that this life was never
supposed to be easy.
Easy like, my brother's high school sexual endeavors.
Anything easy to obtain wasn't meant to last forever.

God did not give us gravity to hold us down
he gave us gravity so that one day
we might rise up.

Without gravity our legs would be too weak to walk with him.
The struggle is crucial.
Without the storms of our lives
our spiritual states would be stuck in neutral.

So keep throwing those darts
at the passions of your heart.
And you will bull's-eye.

This is your full potential.
This is that eight ball in the corner pocket.
This is that fade-away jump shot NBA play-offs mid-90's number 23, they
could never stop it.
Our hearts are copper prongs praying for sockets.
Lightning strike my blind spot so I'll see you coming next time.
Until I realize lightning does not strike the same place twice.
We are unique.
There will never be another like you
and there will never be another like me.

We are lightning.
Awaken the engine in your heart.
Spin in your intended direction
So I
        So we
                    All
                    Can change this world.

8

God Bless You

God bless you.
Yeah, you.

God bless your eyes.
The mirrors they hold
and the stories they've told.
God bless the innocence you've never sold
and the moral compensation to God we all owe.

God bless the skeletons in your closet you chose to expose
and the all-access attractive doorway to Hell only God could close.
But let's not close the door.
Open it up.
Take it outside.

God bless the leaves and the oxygen they leave for our lungs to retrieve.
God bless the trees and the beauty they give birth to.
God bless the arrival of spring going bloom in God's darkroom.
You are the unfinished masterpiece in God's art room.
He is waiting for your permission to make revisions.

But you can't learn nothin'
until you learn to listen.

God bless radio stations that play J Cole and K Dot songs.
God bless the arms of the church that never let you go while you were gone.
God bless your family roots that held you up
when your legs weren't strong.

God bless the haves
and the have-nots.
God bless my Pops
and his taste in Jazz and Hip-Hop.

Boney James and Chuck D.
No surprise the poetry is revolutionary.

God bless my friends and my adversaries.
My hands are filled with penned poems
and dream blueprints.
No room for grudges to carry.

God bless the stubborn struggler.
Always hustling.
Sleep is a myth.
Life is a gift.
Unravel the ribbons and get busy living.

God bless adoption
both formal and informal.
God bless the little girl with HIV aids
that just wants to be normal.

God bless your broken piece glass past
shimmering supernova like kaleidoscopes of hope
holding miracles cradling faith.
Our imminent death makes this life great.

No one lives forever.
God bless not knowing how it ends.
God bless forgiveness and making amends.
God bless the absences of a court room within the cosmos
when you've got Jesus to defend.

God bless parents being parents instead of friends.
God bless the end
of this life and what's next.
God bless not having to guess.

God bless the ribcages ripped by bullets.
They did nothing wrong.
God bless the caskets carried by a mother's song

only four feet long.
God bless the fingers of the forgotten barely holding on.
God bless the psalms from the Lord that keep them strong.
God bless the nails on the cross
and deliverance for the lost.

God bless the broken souls
that know exactly how much the liquor cost.
Searching for satisfaction at the bottoms of bottles
lip locking lies never worth it.
God bless the mistakes that made you perfect.
God bless the Good News
and the first time you heard it.

God bless those ears
the ears swinging from our hearts
swallowing the word of God.
God bless the voice of God.
Bring your ears near.

God bless letting go,
giving this world parts of your soul you never show.
God bless the highs and the lows of our lives.
God bless forgiveness before death arrives.

God bless the story you have to share
and the crosses your back had to bare.
Open the blinds and sing like the cage door is broken.
No need to ask why, when the answer has been spoken.

Yes.
Yes.
Yes.

Your permission to live was always granted.
Even when life is hard like granite,
remember anything worth having isn't handed.
Push along the path of God

even if you don't understand it.
God bless the lights in our lives that guide the way.
God bless the hungry mothers that find a way.
Her stomach is screaming like a burning building,
but through the smoke, all she can hear is her children.

God bless the sacrifices that gave you life.
God bless the candles cut dim too soon.

God bless Emmett Till's last breath.
God bless Marcus Garvey and Malcom X.
God bless Harriet Tubman and my Grandmother's wisdom.
God bless my Auntie's battle with breast cancer.
God bless the screaming stomachs.
Greet their pleas with a gentle answer.

We live in a world where the rich have plenty
and the peasants pinch pennies.
God bless giving more than what you ask for.
God bless the poor.
God bless the poor.
God bless the poor.

Poor in spirit drunk on doubt.
Worlds crashing down,
God already has a way out.
Your heart is a map
and your pulse is the route.

God bless the breath that fuels your art.
Connect the steps that move your heart.
God bless your heart and everything it produces.
The power of God is surging through your spine.
Open your mind like a Bible and use it.
God bless you.
Yeah, you.

The Answer

Hymn-clap a hallelujah into my sky.
Wake the holy from my bones.
I wrote this poem only to find God's fingerprints on my mistakes.

The dark will always fear the candle wick.
If God let your struggle live, you can handle it.

If your faith is a fortress, slight winds can never damage it.
If God doesn't direct the rudder, then abandon ship.

Leave your faith in man
and your hopes will show a pretty cool vanishing trick.
Poof, it's gone like a lost tooth underneath a pillow's roof.

If we are reflections of God,
we can't make a move until God does.

How does God deal with sorrow?
How does God deal with loss?
How does God deal with disrespect?
How does God kill regrets?
How does God silence the trivial?
How does God reach the cynical?

How does God forgive His family?
How does God give light to the liars?
How does God deal with these misers?
How does God deal with control?
How does God reflect from my soul?

My Grandmother Martha should be the author.
She once told me,
"I have the wisdom and the scars to prove it."
I don't have the answers.

But I miss my aunt
while three of my fingers bow to cancer.

Life was spinning like a break dancer.
My sorrow played hide and seek between these stanzas.
Front row funeral seat.
My grandmother didn't speak and could hardly stand up.
Can you blame her?

But through the storm she is enduring.
We all miss Vee like curving
butterflied to curing.
Curing is what we needed when Vee was gone.

Heaven is the next step after death.
The sentiment is so reassuring.
More than a theory.
I saw it clearly through my tears
before they base jumped from my cheeks.

We are most powerful when weak.
My aunt gave me courage to fight
and the strength to weep.

I dedicated my first book to my aunt's name.
The second is for my grandmother's pain.
Life is messy but thank God for the stains.

The truth is most perfect without make-up.
I wanna fall in love with the way I wake up.
I want my reflection to say, "Yes."

Is it okay to miss my Aunt?
Can I express what's on my mind?
Can I inspire hope,
and author books to help the world cope?
With addiction.
With loss.

With rejection and regrets.

Do I still have time to be
the image God masterpieced into my dreams?
For so long I thought that canvas was a boxing ring.

A house fly can't fathom a human life span.
We are one moment blooming through eternity.
This isn't to edify urgency.

Slow down and learn to free the lassoes latched to your "no."

The answer is, was, will be, always "Yes."

Say yes like Andrea Gibson just gave you the definition of hope.

We are all violins playing the same song.
God's word is meant to be your bow.
Shrinking your light is playing it wrong.
Listening to others will lift your lows.
Because we're all playing the words to a song we already know.

When the Holy Water Runs Dry

Open your heart, fill it with the Spirit.
Pray now, wind whispers, can you hear it?
Kill the television.
Lose the trial.
Take the sentence with a smile.
Middle fing...
I mean, throw holy water at the plea bargains.
Don't listen to the dogma they barkin'.
Demons are familiar with religious jargon.
They promise pardons they can't deliver.
When our hearts tremor like blenders,
push forward like you're taking the beach,
because fear is a needed nuisance.
Reach for tomorrow like today is dying.
Close your eyes like the devil is lying.
Start doing and quit trying.
If you love God, keep striving.
If hardships are oceans, start diving.
Hope is the boat you built in a bottle.
The righteous path has sharp curves and pot-holes.
Ease on the brakes and release the throttle.
Like Aeropostale models posing perfect,
devils want us to smile and be happy forever.
Joy never.
Want always.
Always need
more and never stop eating just to throw it up.
It was never enough.
Is anything ever?
If you're looking for direction
God wrote the answer in your reflection.

Your Story

Practice, passion, and proper preparation are prerequisites to receive
receipts that read exactly what you need to persevere.
A friend gave birth to this question.
What happens when your dream becomes a memory?
Jubilation is spelled with eight letters.
Hard Work.
This artwork
has a purpose.
Giving hope, helping you find strength through your own testimony.

Your story is a lightning storm when the lamps go blind.
Your story is poetry propelling into a proverb.

Your story is the supernova that gave birth to the North Star.
Your story makes the night obsolete.

Your story is sonar.
Your story is the pulse to the universe's heartbeat.

Your story will give strength to the weak.
Only the voices from the valley can make our empathy mountain peak.

Your story is an open book in Nazi Germany.
Your story is the broken levy to quench the fire burning our books.

Your story is a church hymn when the hope went dry like a stepfather's
sense of humor.
Your story is chemo for the tumors on our soul.

Your story is like the moon.
Midnight, spilling darkness on our candle-light,
but your life was shining too bright to stop the fight.

Unshackle your soul.

Your truth will set us free.
Shame severs the wires lighting the lamps
in your heart's concert halls.

Take the stage.
Our days are numbered like the last page.

Your goals are Scorpion and Sub-Zero with no HP left.
"FINISH THEM!" Like Johnny Cage with no CG or green screen.

Crash your lies like cymbals with no brake fluid.
Make your dream lucid.

You are capable.
You are worthy.
There are wicks growing from our pain.
The fire in your throat will wake our great.

Speak for our sake.
Speak for the pain that aches loud like city streets.
Speak the silence into riots rising from our unholy patience.
Procrastination.

Practice, passion, and proper preparation are prerequisites to receive
receipts that read exactly what you need to persevere.

Your story.

Open the Door

Your heart begins to beat before birth.
Fifth week, first trimester.
Armed with a message, like a love letter lost in a war zone.
And like love letters lost in war zones
we are all impossible miracles in motion
to this moment,
right here.
Now.

Pull that fear from your throat like an orange peel.
Tune your heart's radio waves to Bob Marley and Lauren Hill.
One Love, above all else
and place those doubts on that dusty shelf and trust yourself.

God buried those passions within your heart,
so why not follow them?
God will ferry your fear from the dark and
into the light so why not follow him
and hold on to hope?

We were made for more.
More than we give ourselves credit for.
Give it all.
Give it all then give a little more.
I wrote this when I wanted to give up.
When you fall down, look up.

Your heart is as stubborn as mine.
It's been knocking on your chest
before you could speak complete sentences.
But everybody in your family was listening.
Like your heart is a newborn start listening
for that first sound, that first letter, that first word.

Be the first to listen and the first to serve.
We serve a God that doesn't rock a crown
He rocks an apron.

Service first, this Earth is cursed if
you don't discover your purpose
and know what your worth is.
This Earth is worse if
we don't realize we're all connected like cursive.
Your value in this world
Is not dependent on what your bank account can purchase.

When I was looking in the mirror
rehearsing these verses.
I saw you.
Yeah, you.

This poem was hemmed for you, tailor made.
Accept the invitation from your heart.
Don't let your dreams decay.
Celebrate life like you woke up in your own parade.

Let the haters throw shade.
While we throw the Son praise.
Open up the door
and welcome in the sun's rays.

Cut your doubts down and yell timber
and find your pride like Simba.
My truth has grown too limber.

Don't stretch the truth, stretch your arms
like warrior two pose and reach
open your fingers like the last prayer.
Don't leave them closed.
Your heart is knocking.
Open the door, let your hinges swing.
Open the door, let your hinges breathe.

Open the door, let your hinges sing
like Jennifer Hudson's voice wrapped in a velvet dream.
Hmmm.

I could rest easy with that notion.
The sunsets of your life are approaching.
Have faith like Evans.
Have faith like Hill.

Have faith and reveal
what's behind the curtain of your future.

Never stop hoping and keep poking
the holes at the top of your mason jar
holding your heart beats.

Your heart is knocking like neighbors
looking for kitchen paraphernalia.
These words are sugar for your Kool-Aid.
Sweet and soulful like they were
poured from the lips of Mahalia
Jackson's gospel greatness.

Goodness gracious my negative self-talk
has grown outrageous.

Quiet your doubts and bench-press your thoughts
until you crack the faults
your foes finagled into your mirror,
they were wrong.
It doesn't matter what they think.

They were wrong
like their essays are bleeding red ink.
The church organ pipes in your lungs are shaking off dust
like Anis Mojgani is speaking,
releasing those notes.
It's a song of hope.

Get those door hinges swinging.
I wanna hear those hinges singing
like a black Baptist church choir
full of my Grandmother's pain.
Lifting a hymn hard enough to crack Heaven's gate
and make it rain
blessings on her grandchildren.
Washing us clean until the pain goes.
No need for umbrellas or rain coats.

I dare you.
I dare you to reach for that knob on the door.
Pull that fear from your throat
and tune your lips to Hallelujah.

The church organ pipes in your lungs
are note-knocking like the sun would speak.
Glorious, bright, & magnificent.
Your heart believed in you before you were born.

Your heart is knocking.
Open the door, let your hinges breath.
Open the door, let your hinges swing.
Open the door, let your hinges sing.
Like Jennifer Hudson's voice wrapped in a velvet dream.
Backed up by a Black Baptist church choir
full of my Grandmother's pain.
Lifting a hymn hard enough to crack Heaven's gate
and make it rain
glory in the garden
of our hopes.
The drought is over
when you open that door.

Impossible

Someone's hope is waiting for your soul to blossom.

Every night my Grandmother is praying proverbs
that I push my potential past the limits I set.
I set bars too low like Super Bowl limbo.
I don't wanna get caught in limbo till I'm super old.

Dream vivid.
Embrace the pain,
it brings change like bank tellers.
If you love your Granny
go and tell her.

Our time is finite.
Cinderella.
For a Klondike,
would you sell a
dream from your heart?

Seams fall apart
when you pull too hard.
Know your home.
Know your roots.
In your heart, don't move too far.
Life is light speed
Jean Luc Picard.
But before you lose your stars
don't leave this moment.

Glasses up
let it breath.
And don't syphon your hopes to folks that won't believe
in your purpose.
Giving your gift is an act of service.

Worlds watchin' - Tell me, are you nervous?
I think my underwear got a little dirty.
Bulux, I don't think my filter heard me.

God did.
Let God
flow through your veins
until hope pours from your faucets.

But it's hard for God to maneuver
with the dead bodies in your closet,
smelling like manure in the sewer.

Don't be good,
be a connoisseur.
Don't be sometimes,
be a doer.
Don't call it impossible,
be a mountain mover.

Move those skeletons into a graveyard.
When fear is present - be a braveheart.

Life is rough like Shaquita's edges.
But it won't stay hard
like level 99 of Tetris.
Let this
be a lesson for your blessings to absorb.

More.
More.
More.

Give more and then you'll receive
the keys to your heart's locked doors.
This is the alchemist searching foreign hills.
Like Lauren Hill, this is for the lost ones
looking for that ex-factor.
You are what you've been waiting for.

Wait, what are you waiting for?
Have 401 K comfortables invaded?
Opportunities aren't given, they're created.
When you make it
you'll have your cake and you'll eat it, too.
Happy belated to you.
Stay grateful and true.
Unspiteful and lose
any ounce of conceit.

When you reach
for a seat on that peak,
just know the humble rise respecting others remaining unique.
Your heart is a map, your pulse is a route.
Questions is - will you seek?
Or will you doubt?

Listen Close

We all have secret sins or hidden truth.
Everything has changed.
God's love is the same.

Can you hear it? Can you hear it?
You can't listen for the call
if your cellphone is flicked on silent.
Prayer is pouring out the midnights we carry like broken mirrors.
You're not unlucky, the bright-side has the darkest route at times.

My sister's life reminds I gotta make use of my time.
She watched devils dressed like angels
crooked her halo like a boomerang.
Snatched from the light she came right back.

So when I'm "down on my luck" I get right back up.
Move forward, the past died yesterday.
The future is sweet like my Grandmother's carmel cake.
The past may be full of mistakes, but God's forgiveness is great.

The future becomes now,
don't wallow and wait for old opportunities to resurrect new.
The present is full of choices
and God is still reaching for our hearts like His fingers are stethoscopes.
Present your pulse to the Heavens and never lower your hopes.

Albert Einstein said, " We all die young."
Because time is relative
therefore irrelevant.

Every choice is eternity.
Discern and see the truth clear like resting waters.
Certainty is a luxury reluctantly requested.
Know thyself and the fog will melt.

Friends value your values.
You wouldn't wear a three piece suit with houseshoes.
Goku can't train with Yamcha and Chiaotzu.

You can't walk with the oldest G with faith untested.
Hope is a blind investment.
That was a lie.
Hope is making an investment while knowing the odds are against you.

The odds are against you.
And yet, you're still breathing.
Like Journey is glaring from the jukebox
don't stop believing,
please keep receiving
the graces God rains.

Give God the reins.
He'll inoculate your pains.
Don't postulate and complain.
Pray true and God remains.
If you listen close you'll hear your name.
Now step forward and stake your claim.

God Is

Glorious, magnificent, forgiving.
God is
living righteous true.
All powerful, gentle, passionate.
Patient & persistent.
Can you see
light dancing dim in the distance?
Closer bright, burning, blinding, sight refining.
Perfect timing.
Love is like
babies smiling.
Love is like
fires burning.
God is pure, everlasting, idol surpassing, worth fasting,
soul feeding, grief relieving
tears streaming, spirit leading, palms bleeding.
Are we flesh pleasing?
Those sins are leaving.
3:16 readings.
Pray unceasing, keep repeating holy greetings.
Following God is wisdom seeking.
Shackle breaking, narrow path taking.
Soul waking, heart quaking, alter breaking, no faking.
Eyes aching watchin' mistaken martyrs parading like false gods
filled with empty.
Empty faith prays for doubts.
Pray for hope.
God is dew drops during droughts.
Praise his name, sing and shout.
Trombone your tongue & violin your throat.
God is miracle's melody.
Yahweh, Elohim.
God is self-esteem, truest self.
American customs, just dichotomous disasters.

Rape jokes, reluctant laughter.
Money first, pockets fatter.
God last, live faster, status matters.
God loves but we would rather...
God forgives but we would rather...
God condemns but we would rather...
Chase after cheap laughter.
Dying thrills never alive.
Dead soon, Heaven groom or door-bell Hell's vacant rooms.
You can't repent or change ways in a tomb.
Tomorrow comes.
Secular alums are just Christian drop-outs.
Study habits become practice.
Pride 101. Envy 203. Lust 306. Greed 404.
Christian Atheism, welcome to the upper level classes.
College debt, deceitful tactics.
College life, no one fails everyone passes.
Like liquor, hate positive, mock martyrs.
Jesus freaks, lynch unique buy sexy.
Sell souls, no receipts, no relief.
Burn forever but look sleek.
New cars, spoiled teens, American Dream,
work hard, buy everything to lose forever.
Regrets grow, we should choose better.
Who is better?
Imposing weather, sturdy shelters during storms.
The truth is refreshing waters blooming beginnings.
Noon never ending.
Grace never pending.
Justice never bending.
Perfect judgment.
Sober your seductions and faith functions over limits.
Limit idols, more scripture.
Why am I here?
Talk less listen more.
Eat less listen more.
Want less listen more.
TV less listen more.

Text less listen more.
"I" less listen more.
Listen for
God's voice.
Through the silence.]
it was always there.

Patient Procrastinator

Living in the belly of His grace,
I awake

to a very sinful and dark place,
and I hate,

Looking at the mirror at my face,
it's okay.

Give a little then I gotta take
these talents on the road and do it for His sake.

Every time I try to do it my way, my plans break
like a California road during an earthquake
I pray
I follow His way and walk straight
I say
I'm ready right now, He says wait.

Wait.
Wait.
Wait.

So I wait
for my savior to return.
Like a war widow
window gazing
waiting for her spouse to return home
from the battlefield.

I am waiting for my savior to return.
As these Earthly concerns
fade away
into nothing
like tabloid gossip.

As the foundation of my faith
grows stronger like a calcium deposit.

Like front doors you can knock it.
But like a freight train in front of a glass house
with snowflakes used as mortar
you won't stop it. You will acknowledge
the passion burning between my ribcage
like the fuse on the end of a rocket,

propelling those same passions to another atmosphere.
And my task is clear.
And it's not to harass or bash my peers.
It's to uplift them.

Because I'm sitting at the desk with my pen,
from the wind.

confessing my sins, it never ends.
So I'll send

these prayers to the sky like hymns
to hem
the scars on my soul that'll mend
when He wins.

Tell the Truth

When I open my eyes,
am I viewing the image of God
or blinded by luxury?

I'm a humble sinner,
God center,
don't leave your holy trust with me.

I would love to see
the money rollin' in like the tide,
kissing the coast of the Florida Keys.

This is more than me.
Much bigger.
Keep the faith.
Nah, nah, eat the faith.
And God will move you forward like a mustard seed.

Don't trust that lust for greed.
It will leave you empty
like a verse with a mad flow,
no hook.
Take a look at the book of life.
Did you find your name there?

I'm not seeing the specks in your eyes,
I'm simply seeing the motes in mine.
Placing hope in the frying
pan, understand every time I open my mouth
I'm simply choosing to be a part of God's plan.
And I didn't do it for book sales or Facebook fans.

I am not a poet.
I am a magnifying glass.

No, this time I'm a gardener
planting seeds
and it doesn't matter
if I get to watch them mature into trees,
dropping fruit for the world to eat.

God
is the chef. I'm a server. His word is soufflé.
Look through the darkness and find a new day
and look at that mirror and finally pray.
Honestly
with no thoughts of perfection.
Because the wisest of us all need correction.
Especially *moi.*

Am I killing the vibe
building the guilt up inside?

Come on, hop on,
Let's take a ride
on the bandwagon wagging our tails waiting for something to tickle our
ears like a county fair ride.
Ooo.
Novelty.
Anything easy to obtain is probably
poison to your purpose. I will be
honest-attention is odd for me.

I'm a shy kid from the block of Beechdale.
Follow me?
And I'll let you down like a criminal
with minimal weapons attempting a robbery.

When I mirror-look
a hypocrite is all I see.
It's hard to see
the God in me.
Lips, hips, oh yeah.

She's well equipped. That's why
I gotta be
prayed up.
These young folks
follow me.

But it never was
all on me.

God.
Yes, God,
has my back like a fortune cookie foretelling the lottery.
Let's keep up.
Fortunes on the front, numbers for the back
we hunger for the act
of true worship.
This is
that new worship.
Mixed with old
cook it in a bowl.
Whether it's rap, poetry, or prose.
"Give it all you got then go pro.
Give it all you got then go pro."
That's what God told me.
"Give it all you got then go pro."
So I'm putting everything I have into this craft.
Always moving forward never looking back.
Haters wanna speak?
I can't hear you.
Why?
You just rearview.
Yeah, you just rearview.
You just rearview.

Durable

Remember the rivers racing from the riverbanks of your heart.
That heart, that never stopped knocking.
Start unlocking your soul's windows and doors
and breathe easy like Obama ended the war.
Not Osama and the overseas drama.
The war on poor, we all want freedom.
The war on skin color, we all need freedom.
Homeless veterans reach out like cedar branches after a hurricane
we should feed them.
We should feed them.
Some shopkeepers keep spikes where they sleep so we can't see them.
Eye sores, business is battle and they can't lose the war.

Remember the racket resonating
from the recesses of your childhood.
Reaching for the sky like radio flyers.
Downhill 'til take off.
The valley will vault you through the ceiling.
To be the hero,
the public perception must portray you as the villain.
Ask Jesus if that walk with His cross was appealing.
Remember what your Grandmother's hymns whispered into your pain.
Those hymns said, "Fight!"
You were meant to take flight.
When those bones dance delicate
like winds kissing canvas on the lips of a kite.
Those bones are still harder than the poems I write.
Fear never had the right to indict.
When it reads you your rights,
strap C-4 to that cage.
This page is a fuse.

Tomorrow is yours - You choose.
They can lock you up but when they come for your dignity, please refuse.

Prison inmates can have good hearts, too.
My cousin is currently serving a sentence like language art school.
The past is the past,
it's time to write part two.
Keep that pencil sharp like a harpoon.
The candlelight in our eyes will dim dark soon.
The only thing in our tomb - is us.

Just you.
The money can't
The cars can't
The house can't
Your spouse can't
Your kids can't
Your Daddy, your mama, your sister, and your brother can't
fit in your tomb with you.
We owe it to life like casino mob debts.
So live life full with no regrets.
Yes, you have something to prove.

With this one life
what did you do?

What Am I Waiting For?

When we grow up
rich is something we think we need to be.
Buying our way into Hell
while Heaven was always free.

Christian does not equal comfortable.
It means to strive
to be the image of God.
However,
if you're seduced by our culture's newest lies
you're committing spiritual suicide.

Not reading the Bible
is like remembering to forget to eat.
God never hid but it's time to seek.
If you felt your heart sink
like dirty dishes from thirsty wishes
then it's time to reach
your hand to the sky like you have questions.
Have questions because the Bible will teach.

Whatever perverted passions are neck-gripping your time
Let them go.
What's more important reading and discussing God's word
or Walking Dead, Scandal, and Blacklist episodes?
I love those shows.

You can't love the world and know God.
Loving the world and loving God too
is like being a Republican and hating Fox News.
It's just some things you can't do.

God was your salvation before you were born.
He was already that shoulder to cry on
when cancer stole your father and you began to mourn.
He was that friend to talk to
when divorce divided your mother and father
and left your family torn.

He was already in the streets,
that salt on the roads,
before the weather channel even saw the ice storm.

He was that hot cocoa from the kitchen
to keep your chest warm.
His love said, "Yes." on a cross
before any of our vows were sworn.

If God is the reason we're breathing,
let's start giving glory
and stop worshipping a pop culture
that's beginning to look a lot like porn.

What should define our Christian norms?
What the world loves should look foreign
in our kettles kindled by desire.

It should make you feel uncomfortable like your foot found a thorn.
Should we 24/7 the Gospel
or be the perception of Christianity when our church clothes are worn?
We've been warned
the Lord will spit out anyone lukewarm.
Give up everything and Heaven is given to us.
Only Hell can be earned.

The courtroom is adjourned.
Start confessing to see the Son's blessings.

A pretty face won't plead your case.
If I can't read, then learn.
If I can read,
what am I waiting for?

Why are we waiting in Best Buy lines
to buy slavery?
Swallow the Bible and go repaint the walls of your mall with God.
Digest the truth and be emancipated.
A man in Turkey proclaimed Jesus as his Lord and savior
and was decapitated.

Drown any vain gods below a sea of Heaven bound Hallelujahs.

Pay attention to where your praise is sent.
Don't worship reluctant or just on Sundays.
Because in some countries
church is held in a basement.
Not for financial debts,
Domestic threats.

Our debts have been paid.
This world is an ocean of confusion
and chaotic waves.
Stop flinging your arms and legs
and get out of your own way.
The Bible is a lifejacket
wrap it around your soul and start living saved.

Battle Cry

Only one deserves center-stage.
The only one without an age.
Ageless auditory author of the Bible's pages.
God invented time so He is not intertwined
within the linear path we walk.

God doesn't lie.
Thank God or curse truth.
Let go or hold on.
Offer your alters
because God isn't going to alter His offer.

The Bible is a book of truth.
God is the author.
Wrote His Son as the martyr.

Died for sinners.
Christ married the church
and yet we mock her
when we lock our
sins in silent and speak proper.

We have to love God on the radar.
Call confession Doppler.

Is it better to eat reality
or look popular?
Is it better to eat reality
or twist the truth like Oliver?
Is it better to eat reality
or manipulate truth
like models posing for Hollister?

Is it better to eat reality
or be a follower?
Is it better to eat reality
or pull a rib from our fantasies
and fall for her?
Everyday
re-die on inverted crosses
and say it was all for her?
Pierce our side with the word of God
and we'd bleed lies.
Two thousand years later we'd have communion.
Are we assuming the union we have with the creator
can be compromised?

This is a curtain call to certain flaws
we insert behind walls.
Let em' fall like flurries before the blizzard.
Faith doesn't have snow days.
Hope spells shovel when it snows.
Hope spells umbrella when it rains.
Hope spells tomorrow when you think your existence is vain.
Hope spells your name
when struggle hangs heavy
on the shoulders of another.
We need each other like cogs in a machine.

Don't leave your mistakes behind the scenes.
Your moments of weakness
syphon strength to your sisters and brothers.
It needs to be seen.

Open your hearts like a home.
God's love never ends like a good poem.
A poem is an edited prayer
and a prayer is an unedited poem.
What kind of prayers are you giving your amens to?
What kind of lords are you giving your Hallelujahs to?
Are you following foolish cues of a sightless few?

Let's worship God righteous and true
and invite everyone from the strip clubs
to the sinners sitting in-between the pews.

God was always the spotlight.
Step into it unashamed and unafraid.
We all have a blemish
but today,
hope spells repentance.

I Know That Tune

When I was ten I built up the foolishness
to back-talk my father.
Not a doctor,
but I know back-talk
is the leading cause of back-hand headaches
among black youth.

Now-a-days the system will dispute,
but my whoopings were not abuse.

If love is discipline,
my father loved me most.
Or maybe I was the most mischievous.
My sister said I was the most curious.
My father told me, "Never bite the hand that feeds you."

Like a cardiac surgeon's fingers
these words found my heart, never left
and still bleeds true.
If this is true
should we feed from hands that slap us?

Should we feed from hands
pulverizing our potential to be human beings?
Would you feed from hands that only value
your sexual exploits?
Would you feed from hands
that pedophile your daughter's ears into sex-slaves?

Should you feed from hands that scoff at your dreams
and demand you remain on your knees?
Should you feed from hands that hate you?

Do we feed from hands
convincing the gift between a woman's hips
is up for purchase?
"Prostitutes are real bro."
But should that be the most prominent purpose?

Can I complain?
Who's to blame if she gets more likes on her IG page
and more dollars a night on the stage than what I make by inking the
page?

But hey! She can flip it, twerk it, work it like she posed to.
Oh yes, I'll buy your poster.
Sign it please.
Friend request, find it please.
Take your time, I like tease.
For the Benjamin she'll drop it like a roller coaster.
Lower.
Please, lower.
Man, my standards got lower.
Want her for her assets and I don't even know her.
Driving myself insane and my lust is the chauffeur.
Strip club confessions, my quote, "I gotta go, bruh."

Was a slave now I spit it brave,
like Atlanta's team.

Can freedom be found
if you burn the picket-signs
that confront the voices that call you worthless?

Do we feed from hands
that equate weakness to a woman's worth?
Do we feed from hands
pulling images from unholy landfills?

A Waco, Texas tailgate company
thought it would be funny

to sell the image of a bound woman
in the back of a pick-up truck,
and didn't expect a negative response to erupt.
Family Guy rape jokes re-run on other networks
like a Prometheus death and re-death and yet
we still bystander our voices holding our guts swallowing laughter.
We need to force the images up like it's raining alarm clocks.

Screaming louder while the world turns the volume down
just to turn the volume up to watch the radio hit their respect in the
mouth.
How much disrespect does it take to make a hit record?

Watching women dance to misogynic lyrics
puts a bad taste in my mouth like I'm four years old sippin' cough syrup.
It's like Harlem welcoming a Broadway production
of white men in blackface.
Why would I swallow mockery with such haste?

Will you feed from hands
or will you free your hands
from shackles and start telling your own stories?

Don't neglect your perspective.
Know your worth and protect it.
Don't let the radio define your societal roles.

You select it.
You select it.

Paint your narrative
and shed light on your heritage.
It's imperative you shred the sugar coats
of his stories' quotes you don't care to live.

Feed from the hands of hope
that helped thousands of slaves
escape master's southern ropes.

Feed from the hands that built your ballot box
so you didn't have to starve yourself to vote.

Feed from hands that empower your existence
and listen instead of being dismissive.

The page and the stage are open
like my ears have no fear.
Speak your stories and the world will listen.

I'm listening.

Wisdom & Information

My poems are chicken-wang, not caviar.
These poems aren't telescope.
More like a microscope
looking for the stories beneath the stars.
A series of small choices make us who we are.
Despite the mistakes and the scars shaped like Looney Tune characters,
we made it this far.

I hesitate when I speak
fearing what I might say.
If the Lord is my shepherd
He is looking for me.
I've gone astray like bullets from gang violence.
But when we ask of America's collateral damage
all I hear is silence.

Light purifies confusion
but it's hard to let go while fornicating with my delusions.

The same questions will give you the same solutions.
New questions equal new outcomes.

Refocus to see better.
Clean the lens covering the iris of your heart.
God is impartial - no favorite flavors
or underneath the table favors.

His truth will never waiver
like my faith when the lens covering the cracks of my heart grows filthy.

The bulbs in my halo need changing
or maybe my heart needs rearranging.
Earth is a hardware store.

But you can't build properly
if you don't know what you're looking for.
What are you looking for?

Money?
Sex?
Acceptance?
Distractions?
Peace?
Joy?
Love?
God?
Jobs?
A cause?
A spouse?
A war?

A reason to live?
A reason to die?
A reason to search for God instead of Wi-Fi?

Wisdom is the Taj Mahal.
Information is the Taj Mahal sand castle.

Wisdom is a home.
Information is just the blueprints.

Wisdom is my grandmother's stories.
Information is a Black History bowl in February.

Wisdom is my sister's testimony.
Information will give me statistics.

Reading the Bible without praying
is googling God.

You have to put your heart into His Word
like the Bible is flatlining.

Yes, that will kill you.
The transplant is fatal
but it's either live in the Word or die with the world.

What happens when living is suicide
and dying is a sacrifice necessary to live?
I don't have an answer to give
but until I finish this book
for now I'll live.

If you're reading this
I did more than try.
Yeah, I'll see you on the other side.
Reborn like the third day.
Every release date is a birthday.

Don't Fail to Mention

My demons don't wear clothes.
Can I really hang this dirty laundry out to dry like scarecrows?
Only thirteen years old.

An addict for those treasures in the attic.
An all too familiar past.
Searching through my father's porn stash like a vulture.
Pitching tents in the wilderness of rape culture.

How can I oppose it when I chose it?
Take the stage.
Recite a poem.
Hypocrite by the time I make it home,
just thought that you should know this.

We live in a world of look but don't notice.
People are dying inside while the ego is bloated.

That spotlight is not right
if it doesn't catch your flaws and expose them.

Forget it
I wrote them.
For fifteen dollars you can hold them.
Pornographic passions.
Did I ever outgrow them?
Did I ever show them
to other brothers struggling?
Same symptoms.
Both the perpetrator and the victim.

"But every guy watches porn from time to time."
Justified by our values in the system.
Women are the real victims.

Caught in cat-calling culture they can't escape.
How is porn related to rape?
Am I reaching or did I drive a stake?
Are we teaching Brock Turners to rape?
3 months in jail for a "drunken mistake."

Do I really care or is my empathy fake?
Questions lead to answers.
Are we asking or masking?

Poetry without truth is a gimmick.
Poetry without truth will have its limits.
Poetry without truth is fuel for the cynics.

These words are petrol-free.
For a while my bar was set low-ly.

I won't act like shame never scratched me.
Reciting poems in church while wearing gasoline khakis.

"Samuel, what do you struggle with?"
Um - I don't pray enough, if you asked me.
Truth, I was stroking like Tiger Woods last night.
If the myths were true I would have Stevie Wonder's sight.

Yeah, kind-of makes you wonder right?
What power does a secret have released from night exposed to light?

My purpose is bigger than a private browser.
I'm meant to write wings on your dreams
and push you from that cliff.
God is the wind to lift.
I promise you'll take flight.
I promise the load is light.
God is yearning for your burdens.

Pursuing perfection failures are certain.
Samuel, "I know your pride is hurtin'."

Secrets lurking Devil workin'.
Darkness all around like your life was directed by Tim Burton.

But don't fail to mention your flaws.
Past or present we all fall like Kanye's single.
Before that Yeesuz talk
I'm talkin' Jesus Walks.
He reached our hearts
and exorcised our souls of that needless art.

Before I wreck my train of thought
let me pump the brakes I need to park.
Heart to heart we need to talk.
Walk the walk, we'll kill the dark.

No more secrets even if they believe it.
Samuel, "Don't fail to mention you've lacked submission."
Given great advice
but was the only one that failed to listen.
Back when
life was track & field and college admission.

Discipline swinging and missing
like Randy Johnson was pitching.
Devilish desires came knocking
and I gladly granted admission.

Watching that computer screen glow
sold my soul in exchange for chains
in exchange for shame.

Gave God the reins.
Now the blessings rain
and I ain't hiding those socks I stained
and the tissues I maimed.
Pants myself.
Embarrassing, but I'll absorb the pain
and give it a name to erase the shame.

Because when you truly release
and let your vice go in peace,
true self-love remains.

I'll Start Monday

This is for the procrastinators.
Reluctant stewards of tomorrow.
A man without faith is a man without trust.
Uncloud your doubts and full-moon your efforts.

Morning never gave up on you.
Dead stars still shine
and they ain't got nothing to prove.
Stay steady and true,
look forward and move.

An inch to a foot
foot to miles
miles to made it.
Never unaided.

Look low to be spiritually upgraded.
True wisdom is never outdated.
Instant fulfillment
will always be overrated.
Be wary of insolent promises
or have your joy raided
by golden-laced lips telling you, "You made it!"
Side step empty words and evade it.

The blind leading the blind.
Assumptions say,"We're moving forward."
When they're really fallin' behind.

If there's a such thing as a straight line
C.S. Lewis asked, "What is crooked?"
What is right?
Have standards to meet.
Have dates to keep.

I've been late too much.
Not a pristine past, I got dirt to sweep.

This is for the procrastinators.
I pray your ambitions grow wings
and your realities become dreams
as your dizzy distractions grow weak.

Chip away at your route until you mountain peak.
Finish the most difficult task first if it's peace you seek.
Any goal that sees the finish line
sees struggle.
Any pocket that bleeds green
sees hustle.

Even if your mother and your father didn't love you,
trying will never be enough.

Only doing,
stop talking,
start proving.
Words and no results
is an empty fate like Marty McFly watching his family photo fade like a
Jordan jumper.

Confidence is locked in your heart's vault.
The truth will set it free
but preparation is the key.

Stop waiting for opportunities to induce your urgency.
Don't make uncertain decrees
and always wash your mouth with hope before you speak.

Peter Hamilton said,
"If you don't stand for something you'll fall for anything."
Don't mistake flying for falling.

When you arrive on this Earth—what do you deserve?
What does the world owe you?
I hope you can't manifest a reason.
Shipwreck your pride like it's hurricane season.
Thank God you're breathing.
Open those hands and give this world something positive to believe in.
Living was never about receiving.
When you're gone
what legacy are you leaving?

Keep Going

You
are the flame on a candle stick of hope.
You are the light cracking the horizon of someone's unending night.
You are more than an occupation.
Keep moving forward even when you've reached your goals'
destinations.
Push through the "You'll Nevers" and the "No's"
until your life reaches its expiration.
Death is certain, failure is not.
You only fail when you've stopped.
So, keep going.
Unkink the fears from the gears that churn
your positive thoughts!
"You can do this!"
"You are up to the challenge!"
"Prove them wrong!"
"You are strong."
Beneath your imperfections
you'll find God's fingerprints.
Embrace your weaknesses
and discover your strengths.
Even if its been 10 years and you've only moved an inch.
I'd rather have a temporary seat on the bench
than to sit in the stands wondering, "What if?"
You da' ish.
So start fertilizing your own grass
instead of fraternizing with fantasies on the other side of the fence.

Let it Shine

This little light of mine,
I'm gonna let it shine.

Let it shine.
Let it shine.
Let it shine.

Let it shine like noon arrived and the Earth stopped spinning.
Let it shine like newborns grinning.
Let it shine like your hair is thinning and your bones are cracking
but after fifty years of marriage the passion isn't lacking.
She still got it, and she know what he packing...
Lunch, for a Sunday picnic.
Let it shine like lovers locked in a gaze.
Let it shine like these words
when I recite them from a stage.
Let it shine like an atheist cancer patient learning to pray.

Let it shine like a sniper's scope
contemplating
a child's life or dead American soldiers.
Let it shine like one versus many.
Let it shine on a few having plenty
while the rest go hungry,
Labeled lazy and thrown into an overpopulated penitentiary.

A forty-seven year old white man
raped his fourteen year old student
and was sentenced to thirty-one days in jail.

Does that make sense to you?
It doesn't make sense to me.
Black men sell coke on corners
and are sentenced centuries.

Let it shine on innocent souls
executed on death row.
What compensation can we show?
Sorry?
Saying sorry is like replanting a rose
upside down and expecting it to grow.

Let it shine like galaxies.
And let it shine on the fallacies forgotten by our fine nation.
Red, white, and blue.
History books paint the picture untrue
with parts missing like the KKK didn't kill people because their skin had a
darker hue. America been sick, someone call Doctor Who.

I'm pretty sure you haven't but I'm hoping that you've heard this:
Christopher Columbus was a genocidal rapist.
It was his "day" when I made this.
But let it shine like God's Son made this.
Let it shine like this poem is a mixtape
and the slaves played it.

This is Harriet's playlist.
Burn the disc before the government
throws subpoenas at the genius and raids it.
They wanna burn my pages
but I'll still burn these stages.
Fertilizing minds while earning wages.

Let it shine like we broke the locks on our cages.
A homeless man saw a starving boy and said,
"This is all I have but here
reach in my cup.
They can't hold us down if we lift each other up."

This is dedicated to the diamonds in the rough.
Gave it all up and the world said it wasn't enough.

We all have a light burning like it's 12:01,

brighter than the sun God sparked in our hearts before our breath had
begun.

When I was four I had a conversation with God.
He said,
"You have a light, so let it shine. You have life
do you really need another sign
to show you that your destiny is divine?
Will you script your own hieroglyphs or let others define
the marks you leave on your timeline?
And don't be fooled by the confines of time."

What do you mean?
He responded,
"The beginning and the end are certain. Show me what happens in-
between those points in your lifetime.
In the meantime.

Shine."

Enjoy the View

The fire kindling my soul is glowing like a moon on another planet,
not Earth.
I'm not from here, death is home like inception.
Scripture inked on my heart for protection.
No Neosporin. God isn't foreign to miracles.
My tongue isn't my own. My God is lyrical.
Even demons are spiritual.
Cleverness and integrity are unrelated.
Reborn from the waters daily.
Blessed birthdays never belated.
This is for my brothers and sisters, we are all related.
We are the breath taken before God kissed our existence alive.
Let's rain dance for holy water like a Native American tribe tethered by
the throat to a trail of tears.
Marching to the rhythm of Southern pride and white hooded fears.
When death is near.
Life is clear
like the waters above a Bohemian pier.
Life isn't linear, steer.
Left right ups and downs.
Have an intended touchdown when you touch down
and reach the runway.
When struggle looms don't run away.
Because when perseverance blooms you'll find a way.
We'll all rest in a tomb one day.
The truth is a continental breakfast on Sunday.
Enjoy it with your stay.
This life is temporary like a hotel.
Beautiful beach balcony view of the California bay.

Enjoy the view while you help others find their way.

HOPE'S ANGELS

PART 2 HOPE'S ANGELS

Plans fall through even when you try your hardest and you throw everything you have into it including the kitchen sink. Sometimes people don't care what you think. Sometimes they disagree and you're alone. At least it feels that way. But the way you feel doesn't always paint a perfect picture of what your reality really is.

You're not always right. I can attest, I don't have all the answers. I'm still looking for the right questions. Everyone won't approve and some that do will ask you to prove your worth. Step up or sit down.

Have you ever given advice you don't follow? Have you spoken of a truth you yourself have yet to swallow? Friends should tell you the truth. So, can a friend be a friend if they really don't know you? Wisdom must be the loneliest word, and the Bible is the greatest story some Christians haven't even heard. I was a decade in before my curiosity began to stir.

Sometimes my Christian practice is like a call to action sentence without verbs. It sounds good, but nothing happens. When conviction is lacking, it's just acting and stale jokes keep cracking the awkward silence to avoid conviction. Not being serious doesn't void reality. The real punchline is that we choose reality with choices. Once one can realize their decisions shape their reality, life can change. There is always a choice.

Even when the towel is on the tip of your fingers and you think you've seen enough, don't give up. Don't give up! Don't do it. Get up and do. Get up and move. Everyone didn't make it this far. Some of the candles held in the hearts of my graduating class where hushed quietly to smoke. Death is a part of life. Weep and move forward. Failure is a part of success. Try again and move forward. The best has yet to come. The only thing we can change is the future. Use every second like this is it. Time is a forever fleeting commodity. It's impossible to stash seconds away in Tupperware like leftover lasagna. Your past is dead. Cremate its remains and resurrect from its ashes.

No Fear

It all started with a phrase that never felt right.
Let's get it right.
It all started with a phrase that never felt right.
So, shall I
get it right?
A friend, as innocent as ever,
said to me, "You know what, Snacks? I don't see you as black."

Look at the way you act
and the way you speak.

No Ebonics while selling burnt DVDs
and you ain't living off EBT cards.
Like welfare means stigma.
Like I mean enigma.

You know, black but not really black.
You're the whitest black guy I've ever seen.
You're not aggressive or threatening at all.

Look at him honey, so articulate.
I'm sick of it.
Twisting my identity up like licorice.
I just wanna fly & be free like Icarus.

But the closer I get to the sun
I'm burned down by expectations I gotta overcome.

Like being black is dumb.
Like being black is a curse.
Like being black means you're guilty
and never innocent first.

Never first, only second,
second class citizen.

I wanna break out of all of these boxes and live again.
But it didn't start like this
with all of the anger.
It started with love
and accepting who I was.
While turning the volume down
on these clowns that would call me white.

I wish I could've turned that perception up
when I looked in my rearview
and saw the police cruiser's headlights.

The officer asked me to exit the vehicle.
I complied, like most citizens
I had nothing to hide,
nothing but pride.
But I guess being black with dignity is a crime.

It was my first offense.
First speeding ticket.
Back then, didn't get it.
Fast forward to right now
young black men still live this
and that is why I did this.

I wrote this poem
while vibin' to a record
composed by Kendrick Lamar.

He told me that
being black is beautiful
and I should shine like a star.

He said get your paper
even though the system
wants to see you rot behind bars.

He told me to tell these
black boys to fly
like Doc and Marty's car.
It'll hardly start.

What you thought was trash from your past
will put fuel in your DeLorean.
And give you enough force to move forward
like you've been sipping on midichlorians.
Fist in the air, we're gonna have everybody
on the dark side before this story ends.

It doesn't matter if your skin is purple or porcelain.
We are all orphans of sin.
It's not always about your origins
or where you begin but where you end.

This ambition, listen before I finish
I'm a take it back to the future
like a Tardis.
And set the bar higher than where the stars live.
I'm a writer for hire exposing liars putting fire on these bars.
I'm an arsonist.

This poem is a lighter.
You are the fire!
Shedding light on issues we often miss.
A lot of bloodshed in the street last year
but I'll stay an optimist.

No handgun.
Six shots fired.
Dead black body.
Buildings burning.
Riots run.
That indictment was obvious.

But we can either
kiss the ring
or clinch our fist.
If money could buy us freedom
welfare would never exist.

Still gunning us down in the street like we never existed.
But this isn't some guilt tactic
or pulling a race card.

This is a grandmother's pain.
Think she's looking for vengeance?
She's looking for love to refuel her heart's engines.
Holding the history
of the infinite lynchings.

This is for the unmarked graves
and the unsaid names
and the unlocked chains
wrapped around our brains
keeping us thinking the same.

You think they saying
Black Lives Matter for no reason?
We've been singing that hymn on our hearts
since Emmett Till stopped breathing.
That's why we in the streets screaming:

Just let me be!
Just let me free!
Just let me breathe!
Just let me eat!
Just let me reach!
Just let me walk,
down my home street!
While they still trace chalk
around my peeps!
So take these chains

up off my feet!
And let me see
my blackness as I define it.

You think you would stand
with Dr. King or Malcolm X
if time was a tape recorder
and you could rewind it?
Maybe not.

Doing the right thing
the moment you're supposed to do it
isn't easy but it isn't supposed to be.
As for me I'ma be who I'm supposed to be.
Quiet, calm, and not always angry.
And for me
that means
Black.

Crazy Stupid Insane

My step-mother's sister-in-law
said this to my father,
"Don't worry about your son when he's out on the road. All he needs is a
pillow and he'll be alright. He's one of those creative types, much
different from those goal-oriented folk."

Being creative
has nothing to do with my ambition.
I went missing
from my nine to five to bind my time
with true passion.
In fact, I traded that nine to five for a nine to nine,
24/7.

I don't wake up to work.
You have to be asleep first.
I don't sleep.
Sleeping is for dreamers.
Not a dreamer, dream doer.
Mountain mover.
Faith harboring.
God honoring.
On His path not wandering
aimless like an oar-less gondola ride
through the arches of Venice. The work is tremendous.

The art is authentic.
My heart is all in it.
My God has no limits.
I'm working to finish my purpose like the punctuation at the end
of this sentence.
Boi.

                                                              Period.

71

Metaphor for:
I won't stop until I stop breathing.
We call it art "work" for a reason.
I got my fork and my knife I'm just eating.

Is there a doctor in the house?
Somebody come revive this poem. It stopped breathing,
killed it game over.
Enough with score keeping I'm leaving
these critics to criticize.
That's ill-advised I epitomize
the illest vibe.

They say, "That's a bad boy." But
I do it for God.
So the flow is never vilified.
And I know, I shouldn't be rude and say hi to those haters attempting to
anchor my wings.
Yet, still I fly.
I'm an eagle in no disguise.
I know those skies.

When my faith found the floor my Lord lifted me up
like my bones were built to glide.
The struggle and success coincide.
It doesn't matter if you're FBI, ATF, or even TNT
you will never blow my high.

This is gourmet, bruh.
You looking like deep fried.
This is Harvard and you lookin' like DeVry.
Go ahead and go back on to your online classes and read the teacher's
guide.
Looking lost in this lesson like your teacher died.
Trick box, I'm alive looking at tiger's eye.

Don't get mad at me cause you never thought
you could rise on up and reach for the sky.

You can.
This isn't
just for
my critical poetry readers.

This is for the dreamers and the believers.
Yes, the dreamers and the believers.
And the ones that never stopped believing that this was possible.
That I was possible.
That you were possible.
If anything is possible
why dream small?

When God gives you wings it means you don't have to crawl.
Get up.
Flying means leaping from a cliff with faith.
Yes, takes a taste of crazy to be great.

So, when they laugh and mock at my pain
and say my dreams are in vain
I tell them straitjacket jacket my brain.
I'm going crazy stupid insane.

Yep, crazy stupid insane.
Yep, crazy stupid insane.
Yep, crazy stupid insane.

When has being the same ever changed anything?

I don't claim to be no lyric genius.
I'm not Chaucer.
I'm not Poe.
I'm not T.S. Eliot.
I'm not Andrea Gibson.
Not even Allen Ginsberg or John Keats.
Release any label placed underneath my name.

I'm just Samuel 'Snacks' Hawkins.
Doing something different; making a difference.
Liftin' spirits. Yes, I am exorcising.
Pun intended.

Did I mention God has all the glory?
If you have a problem with the story I'm not the one to bother.
Close your eyes and hold your hands and take it up with the author.

If Anis Mojgani Played Clash of Clans

This is for bases we raided
and the archers that aided
when their Giants paraded
while my defenses were upgrading.

This is for the gem hacks and the villages we'll never get back.
To the wars we won and the loot we acquisitioned like Attila the Hun.
For the hog riders hopping those walls
like they're the only black characters in the game.
And every barbarian that tombstoned before I could learn your name.

Press the button.

This is for the abandoned bases and the precious resources they gave us.
To the clan castle troops that couldn't save us. To the opened walls
holding spring traps we could never trust.

Press the button.

This is for the boosted barracks that gave us two hours to chase gold and
elixir
and the base setup set up so perfect you had to share a picture.
This is for the 500k raid giveaways.
So easy to get
you thought it was a dream.
And for the last bit of dark elixir to cop that barbarian king.

Press the button.

This is for the Dead Poet still alive
and the bases that didn't survive.

Press the button.

To the clashers that never started and best leaders that never stopped still going whole hearted with a passion that never parted like the Red Sea miracle.

We never needed Kate Upton's chest to convince our fingers to bless our Galaxy and IPhone screens.
We never needed to question what a stranger was doing when we heard that opening theme.
Hoping to sow them in the seams of our clan's family genes.
This for the leaders that never took the jeans off.

This is for Boomaction.
This is for Jabba.
This is for Something and Sonic Boom
I Dare You to think of a Cooler Name.
For the wars we lost and hope that never came
and deserters we could blame.

Press the button.

For the TV spots that warm our hearts.
And the chargers that feed our batteries before our phones went dark.

Press the button.

The Aroma

What does freedom smell like?
Does it smell like ashes and barbed wire falling from the fire on that
poplar tree?
Does it smell like twisted scripture professing unpopular decrees?
Does it smell like inner city death and disease?
Following the crooked forgetting what we truly believe?
What does freedom smell like?

Are my scribbles in vain?
How can they be
when a classroom,
only white faces,
are unfamiliar with Emmett Till's name before I recited "No Fear"?

History hides so seek.
We live and learn,
bodies burn while blood drips from his crown to his feet.
Is that Jesus or Rodney King?

I wanna write like the sun never forgets to rise.
I wanna write like Mya Angelou's caged bird
is singing spring on my fingertips.
I wanna write like God whispered a novel into my fingers
and said the title is "Only Devils Keep Secrets."
I wanna write like I have secrets growing in my soul like cancer.
No surprise, smoking a pack of lies daily.

I wanna write like the world is dark and depressing and I'm emo.
I wanna write like the truth blooms on fertile hearts.
I wanna write like a broken light-switch leaves an open circuit burning
out lightbulbs like a demon's halo.
I wanna write like the nuclear power station's reactor in my heart has
gone critical.
I wanna write like I don't know if I should cut the red wire

or the blue wire
and I'm color blind.

I wanna write like I'm alive.
That last line was mailed to me from me in the future.
I wanna write like I time travel.
I don't know if this is poetry or prophecy.

I wanna write like I have a story to tell.
A story like
we're stuck in an attic like antique armoire.
The last diary entry was blank because the Fuhrer's infantry opened fire.
I wanna write like my wrist never gets tired.
I wanna write like I applied for the nine to five and didn't get hired.

Guess I'll pen plenty poems to bring pennies home.
Just came from Nate, Julian, and Kenny's home.
My brother told me freedom smells like hard work.
Millionaire status if I put it in my artwork.
Everything into it that's how my heart works.
Never an end to it I'm hard at work.
And it's funny when you don't do it for the money it rolls in.
An exchange of worth is natural
no need to force it.
Haters reluctantly endorse it.
The universe is an open jar full of blessings if you're willing to pour it.

I wanna write like time is a limited gift and I can't afford to waste it.
Freedom is bitter-sweet if you ever wanna taste it.
The truth follows suit if you ever wanna face it.
Freedom is priceless,
only slave blocks appraise it.
Like a night club without a liquor license
underachievers will keep the bar low.
Freedom fighters raise it.
Freedom is a race with no finish-line
so you gotta chase it.
I wanna write like Jim Crow wrote

all of history's pages.

Poets, we gotta give em' truth before we die.
KKK would give a nigger a noose and tell em fly.

Legs jerkin'
eyes white
shows over
close curtain
mothers suffer
another dies
a brother cries.

We ask for change,
no reply.
Hope relies on the stoic rise of a reason.
For freedom to blossom it doesn't have to be a certain season.
We're all human no matter what you believe in.
Allergies prevalent, it's perpetually spring in my dreams God bless the
dead like Malcom, Martin, and Trayvon are still sneezing.
Gun shots ringin' like third block is over.
Another black mother is grieving.
Can a child be a child and a solider?
Soul food is poison for your goals.
Did we fall in love with leftovers?

Does freedom smell like neck-bones and chitlins?
Or is it the bitter before the sweet?
It's time to move on and remember what we seek.
What does freedom smell like?
It smells like crude days mixed with new days.
Our dreams have smelled poop-spray.
Now it's time for the bouquet.
Chase the light even at night
and we'll never lose our way.

Hallelujah and Amen

Sunday evening across the table from my Grandmother
this is what she said to me. She said,
"Son, learning to fly is leaping off cliffs
and learning to love is learning to lose
Loved ones we'll miss."

The emptiness will leave the implication
that something was there.
Something is there.

Sometimes, showing strength means
breaking down and kissing the floor,
you don't have to hold on anymore
because God never let go.
God was always in control.
When you were at your lowest low,
thinking no one knows
the grief I go through.
God was the perfect ripcord to hold onto
when rock-bottom was approaching.

All obstacles have been frozen.
When the door is closed the window is open.
All locks have been broken.
Blessing overflowing.
Love overdosing.
It's time for a relapse.
Any shame?
Just leave that.
Positive people populating the perimeter of your heart
you'll need that.
This is God's plan,
nothing can impede that.
These haters throw salt so you're seasoned for greatness.

Open up my book and tell 'em read that.
This is lift off.
Better get ready.
Trays up, seats back,
but the only way we're going up.

The only way we're going up, is when we hit our kneecaps.
And give thanks, because
no matter how broken you are
no matter how damaged you are
you made it this far.
And it's time we go further.

I know you lost your father years ago.
The tears may flow but I'm here to show
the brave engraved into your bones.
You never needed this poem to tell you,
you are worthy.
I don't think you hear me.
you are worthy. You are worthy. You are worthy.

That wasn't a typo.
Cancer can be a tic tic tic ticking bomb in our veins
and it might blow.
So, before the light show,
keep your faith high and your sights low.
Humble your pride.
This is wind beneath your wings to rise.
This is for the crimson feathers
that have fallen from the wings of my Grandmother's soul.
When she lost her daughter
her heart was dying of thirst
but she didn't need water.

She needed her family to call her.

I don't know what you've been through
but let these words lend you strength to

Fight.
Fight.
Fight.

This is for the life in your veins.
This is for the pains that gave you power.

Don't let your sorrows sour to resentment.
Through darkness your soul shines like a pendant.
I know you soul is damaged and worn out like dirty sneakers
but it's time to vacate your fear from the bleachers.

We need you.
We need your story.
We need your testimony.
We are all teachers and we are all students.
When cancer puts up a wall right in front of us,
with our hands together we can go straight through it.

Breathless

My lungs were French-kissing vice-grips.
I remember the backseat of my mother's black civic watching my life
taper.
A chokehold with no fingerprints.
Darth Vader.
More faith in the force,
my God was greater.

Born begging for a breath
breathing was my Achilles' heel.
Asthmatic fish in the water but no gills.
Heart racing but no thrills.
Death breathing on my neck.
Cold chills.

A mother's prayers.
Hope heals.

My mother was praying that the air in my chest was staying.
My lungs felt like sun-dried raisins.

Emergency Room stereotypes.
A black mother Hell raising.
Any mother would.

My grandmother lost three angels.
Look at it from any angle
and your heartstrings get tangled.
Watching a family tree mangled.
We laugh to keep from crying.
But nothing's funny.
Cancer creates more haloes than Microsoft & Bungie.

Staring at that Civic ceiling
I thought about never being 19,
never having sex and never driving.
I thought about not surviving.
I thought about dying.
I thought about not seeing the Grand Canyon
and never being nervous about my plane not landing.
Afraid of heights but I make the hike.
I thought about my Grandfather.
He died in the same hospital I was rushing to.

My life felt like the Russian news broadcasted to Mobile, Alabama.
Misunderstood and irrelevant.
I had dreams then but where was the evidence?

Where was my Mona Lisa?
How many souls did I leave blessed on my Mother Teresa?
Did my heart bleed for those in need
or was it stuck in the freezer?
Was the time spent lost in leisure
or did I make a difference?

I was young.
But how young is "young" and how old is "old?"
What's the difference if time were infinite?
But it isn't.
Death is the finish line and we never know the distance.
If you've got a dream be persistent.
Making a living to live a life you hate living is senseless.

Before your lungs are breathless make an effort.
Make it true before your face is blue.
Everything you've been through is meant to lift you.
We fall before we fly.
So live before you die.

Death is coming like a thief in the night.
Accepting death is accepting life.

Rejecting death is rejecting life
and regretting the sights you saw in your dreams but while wide awake
you've never seen.

In the backseat of my Mama's black Civic
God told me not to listen to the vain critics.
Time is the only thing with limits.
Other than that, the world is yours
like a Nas quote.
No one is perfect, God knows,
but continue on the path that God shows.

Before your body is breathless
and you take your next step towards life's exit
take hold of your blessings.
Because every second is precious before your body goes breathless.

Hourglass

It's time to sober up.
Treat your faith like your baby girl and hold her up.
God's strength will lift that boulder up, that's blockin' your path.
Don't get lost in the math.
God's logic won't make since to us.
My sins plus God's grace equals 0
I'm tired of trying to be the hero.
I just wanna fly like Neo,
But the Matrix has me.
Agents are vulnerable women in red dresses.
Empty sex with a shot of guilt is all I'm left with.
God is whispering questions quiet as a baby's breath.
The answer is what I choose for my life next.

Smile

You smile like a temple's archways before worship.
Your smile is a glass filled with light.
Please pour it from the altar of your throat.
Awaken the hope lying dormant between the bones of yesterday.

You reflect better days
You reflect a better way.

Lift darkness shrouding horizons holding promises of tomorrow.
Like a father whispers symphony syncing secrets of life to a mother's
womb your smile gives us hope in the face of impending doom.
Brighten my life like noon.
Brighten my life like the universe going boom!

Don't give your smiles away to lenses.
Give them to children.
Give them to the homeless.
Give them to the hopeless.
The engines in your heart function flawless when your lips drip joy.
Break the faucets in your throat.
Overflow the cups in our souls.
Fill me up.
Yes.
Fill me up like foreplay.
You take my breath away.
Obamacare didn't stay.
I'm gonna need to move to Norway.
Your smile is the key
and there's only joy behind the doorway.

Cold Blooded

Why are your hands and your feet always artic,
always painting my back burrr?
You must wanna see the lightning crack in my veins
like unprejudiced gunshots.
My heart thu'ums sonic booms like someone in the room is popping off
gunshots when you finger-paint peace along my spine.

Your name means adrenaline in the dictionary of my soul.
You're the spice of my life even though your hands are North Pole.
Touch me.
Reach me.
Breath me in and never out.
I love you, certain and never doubt
a future could exist without
me loving you and you loving me.

Underneath daily routine
are phrases we never say
but truly mean.
Like, I love the way you keep your bed clean.
I love the way you pierce my heart with a smile.
I love the way you became best friends with my sister's child.

I want to reach further.
I want to have a love unheard of.
The world will envy what they've never seen.
Tell me phrases you truly mean.

Spark the dark from my heart,
you gave life to this art.

You are outlets to my power cords.
You are the power cord to the PC in my ribcage.
My insecurities and fears are center stage.
My life is a novel and your support

deletes fear from every page.
Please burrr my back.
Open my pores like prayers.
They're praying for you.
Like the way my granny prays for us.

Thunderstorm my sunny days so my faith will grow.
You love the weather warm even though your hands are made of snow.
Believe in me so my great will show.
Kiss me and my face will glow.
Your love is helium for my lows,
lifted over 60 stories soaring wings spread like jelly.
I don't want anything this world has to sell me.
Find the words you never say routine and tell me.

Please burrr my back.
Maraca my bones.
Ice sickles, my blood drips.
Light ripples, my love sips from the fountains flowing from the faith you
have in me.
May it grow and never shrink.
A cup composed from our souls take a drink.

Planet populating love making.
Toes curl like question marks unanswered.
Say yes.
Floetry in poetry going bloom like lotus trees.
But when I'm overseas, it's you and me.
I don't have all the answers
but you do have all of my love.

Please burrr my back.
Summer day my soul.
Be the light cracking my horizon.
Let's multiply, no dividing.
This love is a cliff
and my heart is diving.
The tide is rising.

Our finger tips touch igniting
the fire you feel on my back.
We are riding flaming waves.
It's a miracle you put up with my binge anime days.

Please burrr my back.
Wake the ruins in my bones gently.
Touch me like moonlight kisses night.
Touch me like the bow strikes the strings on the violin,
juuust right.
It's tuned to the melody of your soul's symphony.
Your touch was the song meant for me.

Three

The artist is an instrument.
God gave me every inch of strength,
from a penny-pinch to a red sun's width.

Are you living to die
or dying to live?
Life is an ice sickle in summertime August.
That's Paducah weather while I'm Billy Collins
staring out the window in my office.
Pass the boundaries but don't live life lawless.
Make mistakes until you make it flawless.

Life is a flash like an unwanted class in anatomy.
If we're all special like Xavier's academy,
other people living their dreams
should be a sight you're glad to see.

I'm glad you see.
I'm glad you read.
Will I ever see mine?
It's only a matter of time.

Two

I hope you can relate.
We were all made to be great,
uniquely gifted with a story to tell.
Every bruise that bleeds helps the hope swell.
I hope you're swell.

We're going up like a rocket launches.
No one wakes up in a dream they go unconscious.
Work wears boxing gloves.
Knock it out.

Work until you stop breathing.
Work until they start believing.
Your lungs are not lungs,
they're harmonicas.
When you breathe I can feel your Blues.
When you breathe I can see that bruise
that your father left,
that your mother left,
that your brother left after his death.
That your girlfriend left when your girlfriend left.

We've all felt that crack in our chest
thinking, San Andreas ain't got nothin' on this.
We've all walked the Sierra trying to hold water in a net
10,000 miles until the next oasis and we ain't got nothin' left.

Praying for a hurricane to wash away the pain
when life gets messed up and tangled up
and starts to look like a Flying Spaghetti Monster.

Don't pray to doubt.
Don't pray to fear.
Don't pray to uncertainty.

Pray like the only language you know is Hallelujah.
Let your faith find the flashlight your doubt buried between your
harmonicas.
Keep the wicks lit in your soul like you're celebrating Hanukkah.
When you speak I can see the shadow of an angel's wings on your heart.

When you speak I see hope.
When you speak I see your stories.
I can feel them - so reveal them.
This world is full of broken people
and your words can heal them.

One

When the top of that hourglass goes empty, flip it like a coin.
Start over like a console reset.
Redress your dreams in different garments.
If you don't love it when you try it on
you'll hate it when it comes home like the shift is over.

Lift Off

Our hearts are metronomes keeping time for the same song, while a war wages inside all of us like two brothers squabbling over the remote control.

How you spend your time determines the outcome. This is dedicated to the faith you found on the face of a penny you flipped into a fountain. That same faith can move a mountain. Every business starts with a dollar and a dream before you can count thousands.

With those thousands of risks mounting
before we start counting our own insecurities, self-doubts, and past failures.

Investing it all to see no return.
The point of no return.
Granny calling, calling, ignore, ignore.
She just concerned. I'm concerned.
Give thanks until your breath burns.
Whatever the soul churns comes back in return.
Will you harvest hate or harvest hope?
God bless the moment your mother's water broke.
And God bless the moment your breath signs off on the last symphony it ever wrote.

You work of art, you.
You move moods
like moons move tides.
I cried until I laughed.
Even on Halloween
live life without a mask.

Tell your Granny you love her.
One day her smile will only live in the past.
And the living cannot live there.

Life is holding on and letting go at the same time.
Don't slip from the cliff
but loosen your grip to hold on to what matters most.
Like your grandmother's smile
and your father's lullabies
or my sister's response to the most vibrant rainbow known to us.

Pictures don't do it justice.
Photos are very skilled liars.
And priceless moments cannot be bought
unless you know an excellent poet for hire.
Don't quench the fires or silence the wires
answering the prayers your darkness prayed for.
No need to say more.
Just laugh & let life launch you
to the otherside.

Crosshairs

Inventors of gods,
Hollywood Heaven home decorators,
taint our daughters with your beauty
and taunt our sons with your power.
We need more. Give us more.
Please, give this world more of what it wants.
Haunt our dreams until we wake to nightmares we've painted with our
pulseless desires.
Meant to please and never harm.
Silence the senseless alarms echoing
through the catacombs of our conscience.
Kidnap my happiness then redefine it
with a Newsweek magazine.

Screen-play love junkies,
let us share your needles.
Inject your decaying ideas into our thirsty veins.
Tylenol our tomorrows.
Hang us with hangovers until our legs stop straining.

Famous for being famous.
Rich and attractive.
Picture painted.
Perfection tainted.
Where is God?
Alter Call.
Reacquainted.
Maybe Monday.
Are we there yet?
Does everyone love us yet?
Please notice me.
Please notice me
like black kids in white neighborhoods.
Judge me like a dress gone wrong on the red carpet.

Punch my throat with Jack n' Coke.
Bottoms up.
Eat memories.
Keep me high.
Roll me up and burn me.
Worldstar my worries into drama that doesn't concern me.
Mountain top my addiction.
Sell my hopes to fiction.
In darkness our flaws go unmentioned.
Number one radio hit my morals grey.
I'll shake my hips but never truly listen
to the lyrics dumped from the heart of a heart-throb.
Okay, his name is Justin Bieber
but a fourteen year old girl's tears call him God.
He sings from an altar.
Some call it a stage.
He's pretty nice guy
until he's caught in a Brazilian brothel acting his age.
We'll never discover the truth about ourselves
until we exit vanity's cage.

If you've been listening into the silence for God's call.
If you're tired of edifying evil
just to anticipate the fall.

If you're ready to see humanity evolve where being beautiful has
everything to do with the way you treat your fellow human being
this is for you.

This is for you. This is for the heroes that never got a parade. This is for
the hours you worked, no one watching except God and your bleeding
knuckles. This is dedicated to your dedication. Only the humble will see
true elevation. No more false gods, only the Word. Whispers on the
wind. Still your mind and wisdom will be stirred like hot tea when the pot
whistles. Sip it slow and God will show the answer to the questions
we've been asking.

Phillip Goodlow

Skyscrapers are prayers.
Let's build a city today.
And call it Phillip Goodlow.

Jolanna can be the mayor
and we can all live in high-rise prayers.
The holders of hope can build the stairs
and the finders of faith can lead us there.

Where?
To the top.
What a view.
Gorgeous.
Stop.
Take a breath.
There are memories on the air
and a skyline of twinkling prayers.

None of us have time to spare.
Don't leave this world unprepared.
Get to know God daily
and stop living scared.

Tears may fall like empires
but this is a homecoming not a nightmare.
This is for the Heaven's and Hell's we've shared.

Together like a family tree's rugged roots
Reaching,
Grabbing,
pad-locked,
into the soil we share.

One leaf may have fallin'
because the Lord was callin'
His son home.
Rejoice! Phillip has found forever.
This life has a short lease.
Release the grief, give it to God.
Give God the glory
and remember the stories
that made Phillip, Phillip.

Even the mayor admits
Phillip was moody and tactless.
But that's probably why
he obtained his top-ring boxer status.

A fighter.
Head-hunter.
Linebacker.

The gentle love that he practiced with small children
paints a different picture. Please receive the seeds sown in a son,
grandson
brother
cousin
nephew
friend
stranger off the street.

Plant these seeds in the soils of your hearts.
I promise love will bloom.
I promise a part of Phillip will grow as we grow.
When we smile, strangers see Heaven glow.

Let's get busy building this city.
Blueprints sent, catch the hint like a foul tip.
It's time to build that city of prayers.
Spiritually fit, we got prayers to lift.

Asking For It

This is for the broken dishes
and the unanswered wishes.

When his fist hit
her jawline,
cracking bone, the law alone
wouldn't incubate an empathic state-of-mind.

They lock em' up
He pay the bond.
Even though her face look like she ate a bomb.
Out too fast,
Autobahn.
Like thirsty hour-glasses
she's running outta time.

Will you give her sand
or give rape jokes a hand?

Don't prostitute your faith for a laugh.
Don't blindfold a testimony
and promise it sanctuary while you call the firing squad.
There is nothing higher than God.
Yet we hire these false gods to hypnotize our lips,
dividing our thoughts from the wise.

We are what we eat.
What are we watching?
Game of Thrones?
Giving soft-core pornography
rape scenes a home.
Do the images we consume
affect the way our thoughts bloom?

Are all questions born with the same intentions?

Why didn't she leave the first time?
What did she say?
What was she wearing?
What was she wearing?
What was she wearing?
Why was she alone?
Why is she still alone?

Why did we disable the fire escape in her throat when the temple in her soul started to smoke like a boat on a river after the fireworks are finished?

We should serve those broken souls
like we're playing tennis.
All love.
No more hammers.
Be the wrenches
twisting tight what the storm broke loose.

This is for the rape jokes with too much air-time,
like gravity went missing.
Should a woman's lips ever have to ask for permission
To live?
To speak?
To breath?
To leave?
To live?
To live?
To live?

Live.

Harmless Questions

Should we ask questions to obtain information we don't have
or should we ask questions to reaffirm assumptions we carry like
baggage?
Boarding planes.
Taking off.
Landing safe.
Same destination.
Did we ever leave the runway?

Why are you so uptight?
Loosen your straps and smile.

If a person is smiling does that make them happy?
If a person is eating does that make them hungry?
If a person is alone does that make them lonely?
If a person is victimized does that make them worthless?
If a person is American does that make them rich?
When the Walton's use welfare does that make them poor?
If a person is poor does that mean they have nothing?
If a person is rich does that mean they have everything?

If it so, what is everything?
And does our current physical state predicate our emotional and spiritual
outcomes?
Is a question a question if it is not seeking an answer?
Are we seeking or assuming?
Should we stop to ask or keep it moving?

A Breath

Every poem begins with a breath.
Then a poem has life.
Like all beautiful things,

we die.

The stars burn out like candles after a birthday wish.
I hope the wishes were worth darkness.
Like those same stars undarking nights,
we all wanna be missed.

Can the truth exist without a witness?
When I'm gone I want saints to see my sins.

I pray reluctant flyers
those eagles meant to soar
while afraid of heights will see
the long nights I pursued passion
instead of pension.
I do it for the love,
but I still need that commission.
And don't fail to mention my fails.

They are nails that closed my coffin of doubts.
Try.
You won't know until you try.
When I die
I pray my eulogy is a symphony
written with the inkwell memories of my family.

When I die,
I pray they say he lived for his "why."
Why do I peel off my skin
and reveal what I feel within?

Why do I reveal the hurts I feel for the women and men
plucked from purity by rape and child abuse?
Battling anxiety and insecurities for years my tears burst like dying stars
for the scars grafted to their futures like their sorrows were meant be.
Society sees weakness in a sheep
devoured by a wolf wearing wool.

We tell our little boys to man-up
and tell our little girls to know their place.
Stay pretty and keep make-up on your face.

When I die.
You will know why I pushed oxygen through these lungs.
It was never habitual,
never a ritual done in vain.
I wanna see God's love rain
on anyone that knows the pain of being faulted
for being who you are.
When I die
I pray my image washes away like sand castles.
Erased by the evening surf
and all that's left is God's work.

Our truest purpose
isn't to increase the girth of our net-worth.

Our truest purpose
isn't to make people different from us hurt.

When I draw a breath,
when I snatch a gasp
from the arid winds of uncertainty
I am not taking a breath to blow out candles and make a wish.
I am taking a breath
to give you a gift.

Thanks

Heavy nights rest on my chest
like middle school toothpick arms curling dumbbells.
My heart swells like a steroid balloon
and sweats bullets that could crater the moon.

Reciting my life through these pages and poems,
slowing the sand in my hourglass to God's time zone.
Work comes before faith if you wish to wake your great.
But for now
give thanks.

Give thanks to Love in your veins.
Give thanks to a life never the same.
Aim for the Heavens in your heart when you pray.
Give thanks for the sorrows that never stay.
Give thanks for the tomorrows dancing our way.

Give thanks to grace when we stray.
Give thanks to mercy when it's time to pay.
Give thanks to this day.
Give thanks to the life the light from suns we failed to watch fall.
Give thanks to it all.

Give thanks to the adolescent aids survivor
and her tears that fall crumbling walls.

Give thanks to your empty closets,
insecure yet baring your soul.

Give thanks to the fear our hearts hold
with fingers of unwavering faith
rocking to sleep worries we keep waking with words of hate.
Give thanks to the God
that already made you great.

For Those Afraid to Fly

Life is skydiving.
God's wrath is ground.
You can't find faith on the plane.
Stop inspecting for proof.
God's grace is the open parachute.
Our souls are sick, God's word is Theraflu.
Prayer partners are soup Heaven sent.
If our sins had funerals they would have one word eulogies:

repent.

God never saw the white picket fence around His image.
Children are scratching heads tugging coat-tails asking
"What are limits?"
Time isn't but we must be infinite.
Love pierces the paradox of time travel.
Can you hear the noon-time chirping church-bells singing?
Can you hear the notes brimming to the ceiling of your hopes?

Stop, touch, and feel
your initials carved into the oak
planted by your ancestors.

When your existence was transparent like smoke,
you were that hope.

They could smell your future cooking.
God was always the chef.
Your gifts grow up into regrets if you don't use them.

Stop wasting food.
The world is hungry for something true.
From Waco, Texas to Paducah, Kentucky.
New York, Los Angeles, and any one stoplight towns.

The truth is found.
with thoughts unbound by the superficial.

Dream of tomorrow when you sleep.
Sleep when you die.
Die to fly.
Fly to die.
Die to self
and serve the pilot who first gave you flight.
He just said jump
especially if you're afraid of heights.

Soft

Expose the wounds
no iodine.
Telling testimonies takes courage
like a lion's hide.
It's much easier to lie and hide
than pry your pride
wide open.
You may fear what they see
But at least they see you.

The Question

Some questions were meant to be born as statements.
Some questions are born answered.
Some questions go something like,
"Do you have any illegal narcotics in the motor vehicle?"

I was a college student backpack full of books, not guns.
Backpack full of hope, not dope.
Backpack full of books
but books wasn't the right answer that day.
Some questions were meant to be born as statements
between declarative and interrogative
because the officer's lips I had another prerogative.
Dresden was the name of the town.
He stopped me because my skin is Bobby Brown.

I was a college student, black with braids, a white gurl girlfriend, and a
'96 Crown Victoria.
I wasn't innocent, I was speeding.
He wasn't listening when I was speaking.
"Do you have any illegal narcotics in the motor vehicle?"

Before I said, "No." I knew the answer he wrote for my narrative.
Another question gone declarative.
My rebuttal was irrelevant even though my relationship with narcotics
was celibate.
Maybe, he was racist.
Maybe, it was for the hell of it.
Maybe, he knew me better than I knew myself.
Therefore no need for evidence because history had made it evident.

He requested my audience on the hood of my Vic.
Digging through my pockets for fossils and hieroglyphs to depict my guilt.
Again he asked
Do you have any...?

I repeated my rebuttal and without being subtle
he asked another confused question pregnant with periods.

Do you know how the drug dogs work, son?
Do you know where you are, son?
Do you know where you are?
Dresden, Tennessee 2008.
But like it felt like Mobile, Alabama 1956.
DYSS.
Different Year Same...

Change

Never Novocain.
Get to know the pain
so you never remain the same.
Get uncomfortable and you'll easily change.

Consistency.

The path to destruction is Autobahn.
We're never out of time.
Rise and shine, shift the blinds.
Let the wick in your throat burn like summer.
History burns,
burn brighter.
History has oversights,
be a writer.

Rosa Parks rewrote Jim Crow's laws into a spiritual.
My grandmother remembers holding those hymns in our veins so our
lives wouldn't strain.
The rain from the storm will flicker your flame.
More of the same or forsake the flock?
The motivated don't know how to stop.
And physicists are still looking for perpetual energy.
I've seen light-speed when I dream.
I've seen God ignite the breeze when I pray.
Don't assist the death of a dream like an ashtray.
Flask a grenade then drink the remains.
Pornography is a sex slavery war stain.
Financial gain for more pain just bodies no names.
Pleasure aims a dart and poisons the heart.

Invest in a life and make a walking, living, breathing piece of art.
Galleries of hope in your veins.
Expose your truth to the world and life will never be the same.

What is this Love?

What we don't know
can it not hurt us?
When lips are profusely pouring the passion of Christ from the bowels of
their hearts
does it make you feel uncomfortable?
maybe even a little nervous?
Well don't.

Christian love was not erected within humble hearts to pass
prejudice, pompous, arrogant, judgment.
Lost souls longing for acceptance and forgiveness are left with one
question.
Where has the love gone
while all of us suffer
from the same afflictions the same addictions?

Our hearts speak but we don't listen.
And I'm the main name to mention.
We can't continuously hum heavenly hymns
all the while, memorizing, ready to recite recipes that reside within Hell's
kitchen.
It's like, possessing the primary goal to be placed on the honor roll while
exhibiting the same behaviors to earn in school suspension.
So, how can it make sense when
we allow these delicious tantalizing idols to vice grip our desire's lips,
rip and unequip our purest truest convictions?
Christ died alone on the cross without God's perfect purified palms to
cradle His cries.
So, how can I cultivate the audacity to grow angry when she doesn't text
me back
or he doesn't call me back?

"It's been like 3 days already
and if he doesn't know the 3 day rule, he needs to learn the 3 day rule.
Because I need attention now."

How, can this be love?
The attention and the affection of the opposite sex coupled with the
pursuit of good feelings and feeling good.
Is that it?

When I read 1st Corinthians chapter 13 verses 4 through 8
did I misinterpret or was there something I just didn't get?

We must identify the true symptoms of love before we can self-diagnosis
ourselves with being love-sick.
It sounds like sick-love.
Pedestalling idols before God, the mere thought is repugnant.
Or at least that's what I wish my thoughts were thinking.
That's a self-perception I wish was true. The truth is
every sin we struggle with and we all have struggles,

especially me.

The pornographic images are pulling at my fractured heart.
But before temptation even begins to start,
guess what.

The Devil knows we love it
before our brains buy the thoughts and we have time to budget or items
to covet.

But don't be discouraged.
Like a hot air balloon made from the pages of the Bible,
we can rise above it.

Because Christianity has never been about what you get
more like what you can give
therefore, we live through service.

And don't be bamboozled by erroneous inferences this world produces.
The maximum pleasure and satisfaction we can receive on this Earth is
hang-gliding our heart's hopes and living for a higher purpose.

And even if you don't know what a Bible verse is
God's love will dance with your heart doing dips and pirouettes like he
spoke the Word in cursive.

If you know this love I speak of speak up
like the world is a broken hearing aid.
Turn the volume up until the Lord calls you up.

Fun Facts

The average American robin can skydive without a parachute.
I wonder what the faith of a peacock looks like?
You use 37 muscles to frown,
22 to smile.
I'm not sad, I just work harder than you.

Sleeping in a motor vehicle is against the law.
That family of four with everything they own packed into their minivan
are criminals.
Is there something I missed?
Most of our laws need changing like diapers filled with piss.

Adults used to be babies.
Teachers don't live in their classrooms.
Student is a title I never want to lose.
Life is an option you can choose.
Death is the option you can't refuse,
so don't rush it.
Depression is a bouquet full of bloom
with no aroma.
with no colors.
with no flowers.
Just "could have been's" and "what if's" and "love me nots."

Stay unfazed by those fallen angels anchoring the pain in your life.
Break a chain and take flight.
Keep praying and invite
those old sayings that gave advice
to the parade fighting your night.
Giving light to heights you thought you'd never reach.
Stay a student and ready to teach.
This is something to lift you like a locomotive's steam,
a motivational theme.

Get to know yah lows in the ravine.
Beauty in the struggle,
that's how you'll live your dream.
Live your dream before the stars in your eyes die young and lose their gleam.

Dream.

Family Tree

Looking for more God in your life?
That's ABC easy.
Communicate routinely.
Between the page and when you pray be Houdini.

Disappear fear and let God steer
like livestock.
Now let me tell you 'bout the testimony I've got.
I've got
one brother,
one sister,
two uncles, gone.
And an aunt, too.
Tears fall, monsoon.

My aunt is a fastball.
I'm a cockeyed pitch hitter.
I miss her.
At her funeral I broke down like a 4/20 swisher.
Now puff on that and let the pain paint the picture.
You would see a flame on my knickers
if I told you I wasn't worried about my grandmother.
I am. I am. I am.
I'm thinking no, she's not a hoarder, she just hates to litter. Remember
she still stays in my aunt's house and I doubt she'd be ready to move on
and move out just because I said so. Because when you've buried three
children...
I'd be out my damn mind if I told her she needs to learn to let go.

She's released enough.
Can't pray for peace enough.
But the lease is up on this house of horrors.
Check my family's aura.
You'd see

Memphis blues.
A melancholy trolley
destination...
I don't know.
Because all we've seen is loss lately.

But through all that loss it only brought us closer.
Is it picture perfect? No, sir.
But when I'm feelin' down my family is there to lift me up like bread in a toaster.
And hold me close like a beer on a coaster.
While I lay a tear on a shoulder.
You better wake up like Folgers
and listen to J Cole cause
we ain't here forever. So you better
love yourz while your here.
Cause we only getting older.
Devil only getting bolder.
Oldest obstacle, better move that boulder. If you're not moving forward then move over to the shoulder.

That last line was from me to me.
Cause we ain't got time to be
stuck in the past.
Pull out that flask.
Fill up the glass.
Give a toast to yesterday
because it wasn't your last.

When I wake up.
I still have a father.
I still have a mother.
I still have a brother.
I still have a sister.
I still have two uncles and an aunt that loves me like God does.
When my cousins wake up they can't be thankful for the same.
This is dedicated to my cousin Lil Gregory, Lil Leslie, and Voijai.

We all have missing leaves on our family tree.
Instead of complaining about the blessings
we think we should be receiving
let's take time and give thanks to the ones that are still breathing.

the Greatest
stOry
ever solD

Homies,

Jacob G and Callon B, thanks for always asking for the next book. It kept me encouraged and never satisfied. I promise the next release won't take as long. Callon B and B James, thank you for the vibes, thank you for the freestyle sessions, thank you for the love, thank you for your creativity, and your inspiration.

Jacob G you are a great poet but an even better friend. Oliver has yet to take a breath outside his mother's womb and I know you'll be an even better father than a friend or a poet. Your drive motivates me. Your persistence reminds me that we are alive and we gotta ask questions and go get what we want. Go get what you want and let nothing stop you. You're built for it. Thanks for the writing sessions, but most of all thanks for being there for me.

Levi! You are two for two baby! Thank you for your time, your words, and your friendship. This book would not be possible without you. I can't wait to return the favor. Before that, Even in Nonsense is next. I can't wait to see where this stroll down Poetry Road takes us next. Keep those Language Arts skills sharpened because I'm gonna need your help sooner this go round. Love you man.

La Familia,

This book would not be possible without God and my family. Thank you Granny, for your patience, for your love, for your guidance, and for your wisdom. Thank you for having faith in me and always checking on me and the status of my hair. You've touched so many souls we'd need the stars to keep count. You were always there for me. Before I was born and beyond I could count on you. Anyone I've ever reached, inspired, or motivated was through you with the love you freely gave me. Sometimes we get caught in our thoughts thinking about how much more we could be doing for others, instead of thinking about what we've done. Granny, your giving heart is an inspiration and a testament to what love truly is. Sacrifice, sacrifice, sacrifice. If every sacrifice you made was a rose petal you'd have The Martha Mountain Range dwarfing The Andes. From the church pew candy to the rent money you'd hand to me, your sacrifice will flow through our hearts and reach generation after generation. Thank you for the Sunday afternoon cornbread. Thank you for the family gatherings. Thank you for the family. It's easy to overlook blessings and in some cases - turn those blessings into burdens only meant to assist and never harm. You always wanted what was best for me even when I didn't want it for myself. Thank you for loving this fool.

Love Keith

Bri,

Thank you for the support and for always believing in me and my dreams. Thanks for holding me accountable about this project and its completion. Your passion for life is infectious and revitalized my passion. Thank you for being patient but always asking about my progress. With the way you hustle it wouldn't make sense if I didn't do the same. This is bigger than money, financial gains, and pleasing critics in vain. Our acro-yoga practice has helped me to trust myself more and to remember that everything takes time and practice. Anything that's worth having doesn't happen over night. Every time we fell we got back up. You taught me to get back up and always keep fighting. I'm fighting. I'm fighting for what I believe in, for you, our future, my family, and my life. Life is fight and just because you stop doesn't mean the world stops spinning so you better run with it. That's what you told me and I'm listening, sweetie. My life is better with you in it. Thank you for pulling through the difficult times and helping me realize that I am capable. Changing my diet with you shifted my perspective. It helped me to be more mindful of how I treated myself and how I treat the world. Friends and family looked at me sideways when I mentioned the meatless diet but it's what I wanted to do. Being mindful of how I was treating my body gave me more confidence to be unapologetically myself and do what is in my best interest when the time called for it. Thank you for the motivation, the inspiration, but most importantly the love. I love you.

Love Salt

Hawk,

Bro! Wasup man. I did it again, but this isn't the last but I gotta thank you for the push to get the first book out. You're the hustler's hustler. Congrats on your seller of the year with H.B. but more importantly I'm proud of you using your gifts to the max and more. You can sell anything if you know the product and you proved that. Combined with your work ethic and talents I don't see a ceiling when it comes to your career path. You deserve what's coming to you and I see more blessing in the forecast. Let it rain and prepare for your harvest. I'm behind playing catch up but I'm working bro, I'm working.

Love you bro,
O.N.E

Sam,

Mansá! I love you I love you I love you I love you. You are love, God is love. For the love of God, do the math! God has used you not only to inspire and fill me with hope but there are countless others you've shown the love of God to. Thank you for letting your light shine and encouraging me to do the same. The talks we get to have and the laughs we share are personified joy. I miss you and Kenny. Watching Daddy bury Vee, Leslie, and Greg put the time we have in perspective for me. Every second is a blessing. A minute together is God's favor. When the three of us link up life harmonizes and forever finds us. Love is forever and I'll love y'all forever. You taught me to never give up. You're the strongest person I know and it has nothing to do with your bench press. You've carried the weight of worlds on your shoulders and your legs never buckled like belt loops. Your life is a testimony's truth when the dark tossed curve balls of doubt down home plate. No flinching with a flick of the wrist your book was a home-run. Thank you for showing me what the definition of bravery looks like. God isn't done with you. I'm excited to see what is revealed from within you. I love you sister girl!

Your Brother Keith

My Makers,

Daddy and Mama, maybe one of these books will blow up like a miscalculated science experiment and I can take care y'all. All I can do is the work and let the universe open, but I'm still hoping. Thank you for supporting my dreams and always encouraging me to go further. Like I told Kenny this isn't the last project, I have too much to share with the world. A light is supposed to shine so I'll do just that. Everyone book is another miscalculation in the equation. Here's hoping the experiment fails and the books sale. If they don't, at least you made to the books to live forever between the pages. Thanks for life and love.

Nothing but love,
Your Son

53529166R00086

Made in the USA
Columbia, SC
19 March 2019